The Beautiful Scars

Aqsa AP

First published in 2020 by

Becomeshakespeare.com

One Point Six Technologies Pvt Ltd.
119-123, 1st Floor, Building J2, B - Wing,
WadalaTruck Terminal, Wadala East, Mumbai,
Maharashtra, India, 400022.
T: +91 8080226699

©
ISBN - 978-93-90040-02-5

ABOUT THE AUTHOR

Aqsa Banatwala, a student of mass media. She aspires to be a great writer. Quite a high spirited girl. Loves to express her thoughts. Her imagination encourages her to reach out to the people with her heartwarming poems. She is also a state-level Skater.

PREFACE

I can't believe I'm writing this book. I never thought that I would be able to express my feelings and thoughts to everyone. It has been a rough phase but I'm happy that my heart has been broken and stitched up back again and my mind has reached to stability. Anyways, through this process, there have always been a few people who have been my strength.

My lovely parents, MEHZABEEN AND PARVEZ BANATWALA, have been such an encouragement in my life. You make me believe that nothing is small or big and one can achieve anything he wants in life with sheer determination and passion. You guys are my lucky stars. I love you infinity and beyond.

"A Brother is what a best friend can never be".Indeed, a bond between siblings is the most enduring bond which one has. I would also like to thank my brother AZHAR BANATWALA for motivating me and making me realise that anything is possible.

Thank you, Miss Audrey Miranda, for boosting my

morale and pushing me out of my comfort zone to help me grow in the field I'm interested in.

Many thanks to my grandparents for showering me with their blessing.

There is no vocabulary for love within a family. Thank you to my lovely big family, for all your love and support.

A special thanks to Sameer Ambildhok, my Project Manager, Pranali Naidu, and the entire team of BecomeShakespeare.com for investing their time and efforts and helping me achieve my dreams.

I would like to thank my friend, Vrichi Shah for bringing my poetry's to life with her wonderful illustrations.

CONTENTS

THE WAIT

Standing in the dark, waiting for him to come back,

With bruises all over my body, and hope in my heart,

But all I could see were his fading footprints, slowly
disappearing along with the darkness

never turning their way back to my hopeless expectation.

LET GO

Asking him not leave me there alone in this
ferocious world,

With these monsters all around, escaping from the
clutches of the society,

running & finding my way back to him, begged him

not to go but all he did was let go.

AND I LOVE YOU…!

Never knew you would mean this much to me when
we first met,

Couldn't take my eyes off you, all your flaws
complemented mine, It suited me just fine.

It was just you all around, other than that there were
no bounds,

Only if you know how much it means,

To be with you is a dream.

I LOVE YOU.

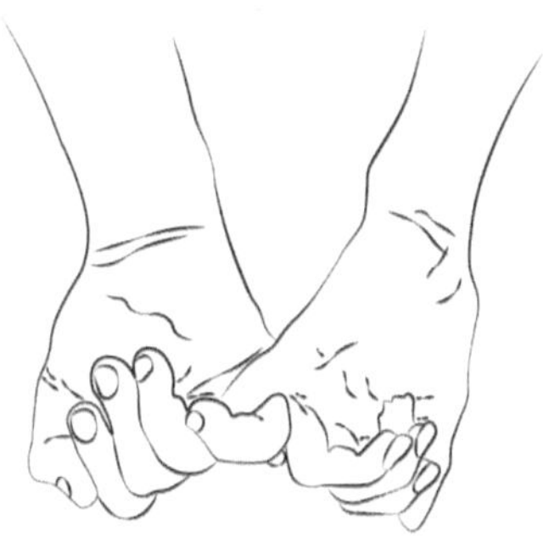

I MISS YOU

Turning and tossing in my bed, my eyes going red,

crying to myself at night, the loss was not just right,

Wishing you were here by my side, only to span the tide,

just want to relive all those moments with you once again,
and throw away all the pain,

What am I supposed to do without you, when I am
asking god to bring me back to you.

SCARS

Fading lights, messy hair

Ran to escape the horrifying air,
with tears in her eyes which knew
no bound,

All around there was no sound,

Despair and disgust in herself
surround,

The sorrow here in leaps abounds,

Drowned herself in the midst of
the night,

Love was gone without a fight.

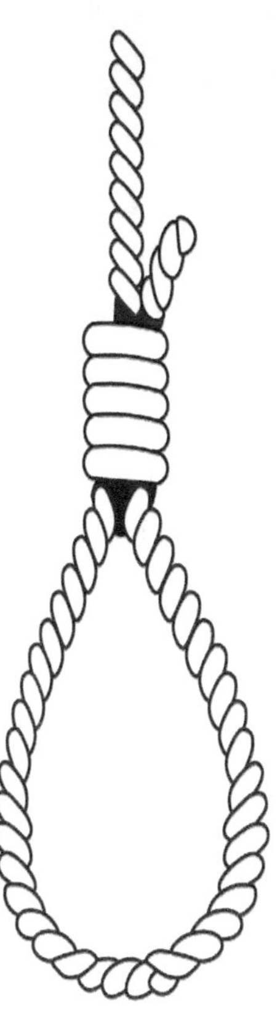

DEPRESSION-My One & Only Friend

A tragic phase in everyone's life, without it no one survives,

A loss too heavy to bear, all around with tears I stare,

Been there with me throughout my petrified phase,

It is in silence that I gaze,

Can't you just stop the chase?

Life is one hell of a race.

RAIN

And there you were, with arms wide open,

Time with you had no notion,

the wild rain hitting your face, tears rolling down your cheeks,

I braved the winds and lightning streaks.

Still longing for me to come back,

But all I could do was fill in the empty racks.

Feelings still run high,

To run & embrace in your warmth anigh.

NO CARE

Dancing to the music, with a wine glass in his hand,

Not caring about the world, enjoying in his own la la land.

Down with all tension and strife,

Life is a bliss without power and might.

MEMORIES

Turning all those nights into mornings, fights into confessions storming,

Tears into giggles, with you gone,

There is nothing more for which I long…!

IT'S OKAY

It's okay to cry, it's okay to be clumsy,

It's okay to feel the pain, it's okay to get hurt,

It's okay to act weird,

It's okay to be you,

The world should be able to accept you with your flaws & not change the way you are,& if they do then they are not right for you.

SUN & MOON

When the sun sets, the moon creeps in,

And darkness I am left within,

leaving it there alone to face the world,

who cares for me not one,

Making the night shine like gold, just don't go,

Or else lets make the night like old.

DARKNESS

Darkness all around, no way to escape the grounds,

With demons grasping you by hair, clothes burned
down with flare,

Pleading to have mercy, couldn't escape the conspiracy.

MINE

Seeing you walk down the asile, with your friends
waiting for a while,

staring at me with those sweet innocent eyes, could
feel the emotional vibe,

That is when I knew you were completely mine.

HATE

All those precious funny moments, suddenly turned
into hate as

You said there is no time to waste.

DEPRESSION II

Comes way to fast and leaves gradually, hurts you but
moulds you

I trip when I care,

How much can I bear?

No one cares.

BROTHER

Amazing nights, childish fights,

Innocent faces, smiles with braces,

Oh how blessed I am to have a brother in my life,

One will never know, how it pleases me so.

STARS

The stars reminds me of those beautiful hours,

Which we spent behind those bars,

Where you proposed me with those wonderful flowers,

That moment was ours.

DECEIVED LOVE

Trying to justify what you had done,

When all you had was lust,

Making me hard to trust,

Making me question every single thing about you,

Cause now I know that there exists Cheaters like you.

When you not only broke you but also me.

LIFE

Why is life so unfair, leaves us with no care,

Just a flip of seconds,& all you see is gone, even if you beckon,

Making us question why?

Leaving us there dumb founded with a sigh.

GONE

Just get out of my head, let me get out this mess,

Why are you still here, when you're gone,

Can't you just leave me alone,

Take all the memories with you when you're gone,

You proved me right that in trusting you I was wrong.

JUDGE

The world will judge you no matter what, no

Matter how many times have you proved yourself,

They won't accept the fact, it's their job to judge you &

You're job to say fuck you.

WHY?

You knew I was afraid to love, made me fall in love
again,

Gave me a thousand reasons to trust & love,

Poured my heart to you &

All you did was bid adieu.

SAVE

People say save, but they don't know
　　what happens in the cave,

　　　They can't relate,

With all those bodies lying
　　　frozen there,

　　Begging for help &

Fighting for themselves.

HOPE

Sitting at the window, staring at the sky,

Once again hoping you would be here by my side,

Why is it so difficult to let you go?

Why is it so difficult to not miss you anymore?

FORGET

Forgotten and moved on,

Yet the streets remind me of us,

The faint smells of the beautiful lilies, reminds how
we used to be,

The echo's of the sounds still Say we were meant to be,

Miss those days where it was just you and me.

HEART BREAK

Was it too early to say good bye,

Cause Seeing you with her makes my heart ache,

You were my first ever heart break,

And now I want you back all to myself,

but all I can I say is 'all the best' with a fake smile on my face.

ESCAPE

Let me escape to where I can lead a happy life,

Just let me go far away,

Far away from the city,

Where I am me, myself

Let me find myself back.

NO LOVE

I don't think I'll be able to love again, you're still
stuck in my brain,

Remember the last time when we met,

In the middle of the heated argument,

you just stood up and went,

tripping, falling, ran behind you

caught my breath and screamed your name,

but you paid a deaf ear to my screams & just fled
never to be seen again.

STRANGER

Just a normal stranger walking through the woods,

Along with a camera and just few dollars in his pocket,

Trying to capture all the beautiful moments, not
knowing where the path will lead him,

But having faith in god and looking forward to
explore/unfold his unknown destiny.

NO HATE

I don't hate you, I hate what you did to me,

Pretended to be mine, when all you could see was her,

Intertwined with her, Thinking I was fine,

Left me there all alone, for her,

Cause she was your main now,

While I was your discovered remains.

PLEASE LEAVE

And then you come back to me saying "SORRY"

Thinking everything will be merry,

Nothing can change because I'm happy now,

Can you please leave without me taking a bow.

ULTIMATE ETERNITY

Miles to go, away from home,

To the place where angels dance and demons roar,

Where one meets their soul,

Where right is right and wrong is wrong,

Waste no time anymore, let's just go,

Where it's just me and my eternity.

NO HOLDING BACK

So what if he goes, you're whole life has been a lie
with him around,

Let him go, don't hold back,

getting him into your life was fallacious,

but abolishing him from your life will be victorious.

HOW?

In solitude I cry, in bliss I feel you,

How is it even possible for you to move on so easily?

Not even thinking about me, us.

HAPPY LIFE

Now that when I know I'm better off without you,

I'll make sure to conduct a happy life and not cry over you.

PAIN

I wish I never knew that guy,

who caused all the miseries and pain,

Left me in vain.

I'M NOT OKAY

Everyone is asking me how am I doing?

With a smile I reply "amazing"

But how do I make them hear my heart cry,

Making my soul scream,

wishing all this was

just a dream

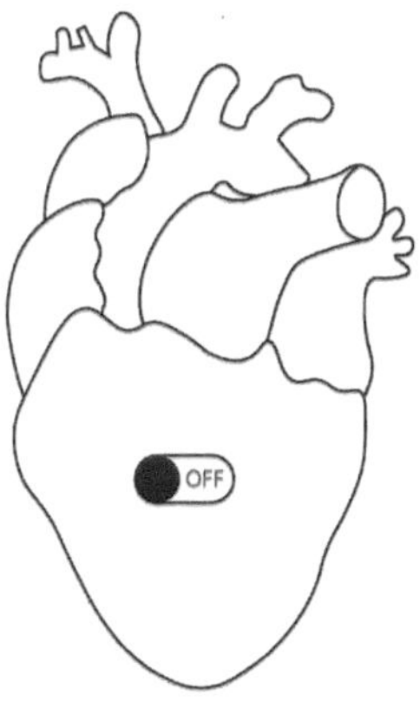

FADED

Love fades, memories don't,

With each approach, they get stronger,

Making everyday stretch a little longer.

BACK LIKE BEFORE

I still love you, I still feel you

the thought of losing you still makes breaks my heart,

there is nothing I can do except to disregard you,

but still wanting you to come back as a new you as
never before.

I DON'T

Waiting for you at the spot we had made memories,

Hoping for you to appear again in these hazy, blurry
moments of my life,

Want to start over with you but I can't,

Because I love you but don't want you.

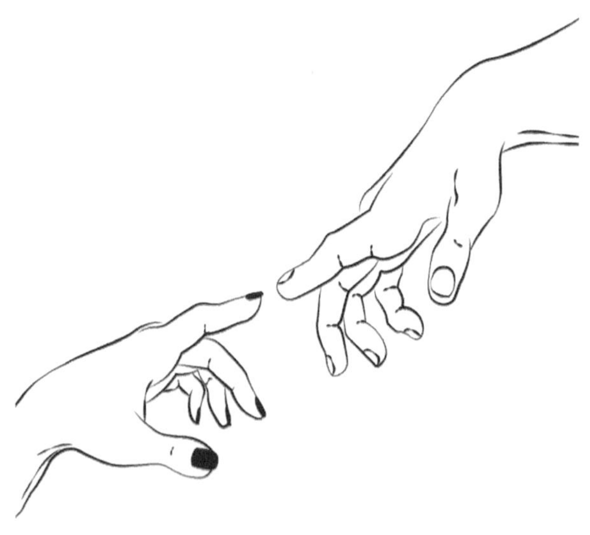

WITH ME

I can't move on without You, need you by my side,

Giving me a ride,

Escaping from this mess, to pass this test.

GOOD BYE

But you are not sober neither am I,

You are not over neither am I,

But it is time to say good bye.

BY MY SIDE

Don't know how to handle this mess,

But as long as you are there we will.

There is nothing to fear,

When you are near,

Though the seas are rough,

We will be tough.

FAKE PROMISES

I can't keep making false promises,

When I know

My heart belongs to the one who I have loved so.

JUST FRIENDS

I love you, I want you,

I need you, but I can't hurt you,

I tried but I can't be more than friends with you.

The times have passed,

And we remain friends apart.

DISASTROUS LIFE

Why did this life choose me,

Made me loose me, who am I can someone tell?

Cause it might ring a bell,

Because I'm trying to flee from hell.

STILL FOREVER

Let's all go back to the moment when I realized I truly loved you,

Decided never to leave, wishing it was perpetuity,

What a happy and blissful moment to be by your side,

Heart beats pulsing as we ride,

It is always a moment which I still bide.

US

Running back into your arms, being embraced in your warm hug,

Forgetting everything, no one to bug,

And you whispering "don't worry, I promise its us forever",

Reassumes me of your firmness ever.

MUST

I want you to hold my hand, till the most special day
of my life,

Vow on the verge of a knife,

To finally make us, which will forever be a MUST.

ALIVE

Still have sleepless nights, imagining you by my side,

Those small special moments which made me feel alive,

You were my boo,

I don't want you but I want you too.

FOOLISHNESS

People say he was a fool to loose a girl like you,

I agree you were a fool,

But how do I tell them that how much a fool I am

to still hope for a future with you.

I'M SORRY

I'm sorry but I can't use you,

Be the one to fool you,

You were my staff to hold on,

I can't hurt you,

Not pain you,

I just can't put you in the same position as me before,

Nor be fooled by you,

I must let you go, and live my life as before.

WHY CANT I?

I don't know why am I still lonely,

Even when he is holding me so closely,

Despite of having new arms around me,

Be the wanna be,

Why can't I have the same thing with him

Nor be fooled by you,

I don't have any clue,

Maybe my love is not

Over for you.

MOVE ON

And yes we are broken,

We are hurt,

Can't live like this our whole life, have to move on,

Overcome the pain, emerge as the one we were
before all this,

Be the warrior, and not a carrier.

STAND STRONG

Memories haunt, mocking taunts,

It is easy to rot rather than stop,

But more easy to face it,

And make the little bit lit.

CONFUSED LIFE

Life won't be so confusing,

If we got everything on a plate,

If we were each other's best mate,

Then there would be none to bait.

DARK LOVE

Love is hideous,

Hollow and deep,

only the dark parts are the ones where one can peep,

not the sweetest ones.

FOR YOU

For you I'll fight against the world, I'll fight against myself,

Make a courageous move with every breath,

Baby, it's Only for you.

NO COME BACK

How much ever I try to bring you back

but

there is no come back.

CHEATING

World is full of cheaters, being a part of the predators,

I never knew,

Until I met you.

ONLY WAIT

With the smile I can't have back, with the roads I
can't take,

With the moves I can't make,

Can't do anything except to wait.

BLIND LOVE

Loved you,

Realized love is blind,

And when I'm awake, I found you fake.

NOT WORTHY

And you made me look fake,

It was my love,

not a piece of cake.

IMPORTANCE

Never knew someone who didn't mean anything,

Could mean so much, give your cheeks a natural kind
of blush,

Making you my new crush.

THANK YOU

Oh god thank you sending your messenger as

a stranger,

who made me realize the danger.

WHO ARE YOU?

Who are you?

Are u the person that came during my worst days and
made me feel alive?

Are you the person who understood me when nobody
else could?

Are you the person who loved me when I didn't even
love myself?

Are you the person who gave me hope, when I had
lost it all?

On a second thought are you the person

For whom I can risk it all?

MAD LOVE

You should be glad,

That she had loved you like mad.

NEW WORLD

Waited for you,

letting go of the memories a few,

cause I knew how you blew,

And wanting to start a world of new.

HOPE

I thought you would never let my heart break,

Cause you were my love no one could take,

But now the future we can't make,

Cause your love is fake.

RARELY

To find love like this very rare,

Where it's just you and your mare,

To loose a love like this no one dares.

RAINS

Making memories in the rain,

Never felt the pain,

Until you left me there in vain.

MASTER

It's just a phase,

And you have no option but only to gaze,

Accomplishing the dreams you have to chase,

to prove,

That you're the Master of this maze.

TO DIE

Why can't I,

See the world with my eye,

Tell everyone goodbye,

And feel as if all of this was a lie,

But the truth makes me cry,

As very soon I was to die.

www.ingramcontent.com/pod-product-compliance
Lightning Source LLC
Chambersburg PA
CBHW021336160726
47994CB00007B/2728